THE HORSEMEAT COOKBOOK

Braising Saddles and other recipes

THE HORSEMEAT COOKBOOK

Braising Saddles and other recipes

⬚ SQUARE PEG

Published by Square Peg 2013

2 4 6 8 10 9 7 5 3 1

Text by Chris Windle

First published in Great Britain in 2013 by
Square Peg
Random House, 20 Vauxhall Bridge Road,
London SW1V 2SA
www.vintage-books.co.uk

Addresses for companies within The Random House Group Limited
can be found at:www.randomhouse.co.uk/offices.htm

The Random House Group Limited Reg. No. 954009

A CIP catalogue record for this book is available from the British Library

ISBN 9780224098540

The Random House Group Limited supports The Forest Stewardship
Council® (FSC®),the leading international forest certification
organisation. Our books carrying the FSC label are printed on
FSC® certified paper. FSC is the only forest certification scheme
endorsed by the leading environmental organisations, including
Greenpeace. Our paper procurement policy can be found at
www.randomhouse.co.uk/environment

Typeset in Bembo by Carrdesignstudio.com
Printed and bound by CPI Group (UK) Ltd, Croydon, CR0 4YY

CONTENTS

Introduction

HORSEMEAT – AND WE'RE OFF!

'There is something about the outside of a horse
that is good for the inside of a man.'

Winston Churchill

Okay, so Winston may not have been talking literally, but he
was on to something. Horsemeat is good for us: it's leaner, less
calorific and cheaper than beef. It also tastes nice. The problem
is, when it comes to horses, we Brits are a bit messed up. We'll
eat like one but refuse to countenance actually eating one.

In essence, the only reason the horse has been elevated above
other species, such as cattle, is because, depending on the breed,
it's either really good at pulling a carriage or very fast over a jump.
We associate them with romantic notions of rustic life, involving

flat-capped men and shaggy carthorses; gliding powerfully around a race track; or being ridden by kings into battle. Shakespeare barely lifted a quill without mentioning the animal and national treasure Clare Balding once wrote, 'I didn't just grow up with horses, I wanted to be one,' adding that as a girl she'd often bring her first Shetland pony into the kitchen since it was 'part of the family'. Which is obviously something we can all relate to.

They are our friends and workmates and have sacrificed themselves for our freedom on the world's battlefields. Clearly, there is no way *Black Beauty* would have captured so many children's imaginations if it was about a lumbering dairy cow.

So when the nation discovered its supermarkets were brimming with burgers containing added salt and Shergar, and that sorry beasts were being shunted illegally around dodgy abattoirs in the dead of night, it reared up on its back legs and whinnied with disgust. It was as if our very own grandparents had been put through the grinder. There was justifiable horror that food labels couldn't be trusted – and less rational disquiet that someone might have eaten the very creature they'd spent many happy childhood hours learning to ride on.

But there is a silver lining to this equine cloud. Horsemeat has hurdled into the spotlight, finally whipping up some much-needed publicity in the UK and piquing the interest of more adventurous meat eaters.

Compared to our European friends we have a long way to travel when it comes to filly feasting. It is, surprisingly, the Belgians, who consume the most per person at just over 1kg a year. They are closely followed by the Dutch and Italians, with stereotyped horse-munchers, the French, unable to muster even half a kilogram. The shame!

According to France's horsemeat trade body Interbev Equins, the meat's popularity is back on the rise after years of decline and they do still knock back 20,000 tonnes of the stuff each year. But that's half as much as the Italians wolf down – it's no wonder they can't produce any decent racehorses.

In Britain we eat about as much guinea pig as we do horse, which is to say hardly any at all unless it's in a microwaveable beef lasagne or we're on holiday. But a recent Ipsos MORI poll found that one in three of us would be happy to eat horse as long as it came from a well-regulated supplier. If that's you, welcome! You've come to the right recipe book.

A recipe for a horse

This book is designed to open the stable door to a world of equine culinary opportunities. It takes a canter through classic European horsemeat recipes and favourite family dishes that can be transformed into gamey wonders by ditching Daisy or Porky and giving Dobbin some time in the oven. It then saddles up for a trip around the world's pre-eminent horse-eating cultures, discovering how they fill their stomachs with the beloved beast.

You'll quickly find it's not just the French and Italians that are partial to pony. The Japanese and Koreans, for example, are keen Ned nibblers. And they like it raw. Which adds another level of squeamishness to an already challenging dining concept. For someone taking their first steps in equine cuisine, gulping down Yuk Hui – that's a Korean raw horse salad – might prove a little intimidating. Then again, it might be the start of a foodie love affair that finds them attempting to take bites out of passing police horses.

If you're keen to introduce friends to something exotic, *beshbarmak* would be a safer call. The ancient Kazakhstani horse and mutton dish is served on thick noodles accompanied by a spicy sauce. Traditionally Kazakhs decorate their table with a sheep's skull, so if you can find a spot for one then you'll really be eating in style. Ideally it should sit next to the most respected member of the group – although they may not take it as the compliment it is meant to be.

Horsemeat also graces the dining tables of French Canada, Tonga, Mongolia, Iceland, Sweden, Russia and Indonesia, among others, and you'll find this reflected by the recipes included in this book. That's a lot of people who'll happily eat Frankel and his chums.

For those who prefer simple meaty pleasures, horse is no cheap substitute. This book's steak and roast recipes are designed to let its tender flavours do the talking, while home cooks wishing to show off their cheffing skills can turn their hands to fashionable kitchen techniques, including smoking horse in hay, where it should feel right at home.

Horsemeat in Europe – a brief history

The western world's attitude to horsemeat began turning sour back in the 8th century, which is a relatively recent shift in perspective considering horse and human have been sharing the planet for thousands of years.

Pope Gregory III can take a lot of credit for giving it a bad name. In 732 he decided to strike a blow against those ungodly Germanic pagans by banning their habit of slaughtering and eating horse. In a letter to Saint Boniface, his man in charge of spreading Christianity into the darkest parts of the Frankish Empire, he told him to:

'Suppress it in every possible way with the help of Christ and impose a suitable penance upon offenders. It is a filthy and abominable custom . . . We pray God that . . . you may achieve complete success in turning the heathens from the errors of their ways.'

Obviously Gregory would never have made such a decree if he'd put his foodie prejudices aside for a moment and tried a delicious horsemeat fajita. But he didn't give it a chance and instead began a culinary crusade that condemned horse-eaters to centuries of furtive filly munching. Furthermore, as Christianity spread north into Scandinavia, previously enthusiastic equine cooks began having second thoughts.

Luckily for the nomadic peoples of central Asia the Pope's influence didn't stretch that far east, which meant they could continue tucking in. It is said that Mongolian horsemen used to tenderise their steaks by putting them under their saddles while they rode, which shows an impressive commitment to fine dining. Others say it was actually a way of soothing saddle sores on a horse's back, but let's not let that ruin a good story.

It wasn't until Napoleon Bonaparte started throwing his weight around Europe that parts of the western world once again began eyeing their horses and salivating. During the Napoleonic Wars, French troops often found themselves in tricky culinary situations. It was, after all, almost impossible to get a good meal during a siege. It's also extremely hard to properly enjoy a long lunch, which is every Frenchman's right, when someone is trying to lance you with a bayonet.

Baron Dominique-Jean Larrey, the French army's chief surgeon, advised troops to eat their horses rather than succumb to starvation, which led to stallion-stewing scenes during battles such as the siege of Alexandria in 1801 and at Aspern-Essling in 1809 when troops are said to have fried up horseflesh using the breastplates of their fallen comrades. Obviously Larrey was no barbarian and didn't expect the men to consume anything over-cooked or under-seasoned. They weren't British.

Still, eating horsemeat remained illegal in France until 1866, despite the fact hard-pressed Parisians would regularly serve up the animal as a cheaper alternative to beef and pork. It wasn't until another conflict that the trend really took hold.

During the Franco-Prussian War of 1870-71 Paris was besieged and the locals were hungry. They were also slightly peeved that the horses were gobbling all the grain. So they ate them, ravenously. There were even unconfirmed reports that people with long faces were being mistakenly thrown under the grill.

Now horse wasn't just food for the poor; everybody, even literary greats, were surviving on it. In *The Memoirs of Victor Hugo* the *Les Misérables* author wrote on 22 October 1870, 'We are eating horsemeat in every style'. And he penned a poem declaring that he would send a 'cooked wing of Pegasus' to an actress he was pursuing who had turned down his invitation to dinner, demonstrating the remarkable rise of horsemeat from illicit belly filler to luxury food of seduction.

At around the same time, over in Metz, Auguste Escoffier, the man who went on to become known as the King of Chefs, was cutting his cordon bleu teeth while treating the army's top brass to horsemeat during another siege. As rations ran low he began

Horse sir? No thanks I'm a Victorian

February 6 1868 was supposed to be the day that horsemeat took its place alongside beef and pork in Britain's culinary consciousness. The scene was set. MPs, doctors, scientists and journalists – the decision makers and opinion formers of the day – had gathered at London's Langham hotel for a Banquet Hippophagique. Or, as others termed it, the Great Horse Dinner.

The Victorian traveller and antiquarian, Algernon Sidney Bicknell, was the brains behind the operation. Against the background of a recent foot-and-mouth outbreak and malnutrition among London's poor, Bicknell was convinced the time was right to launch this cheap yet healthy wonder meat on the nation. He was wrong.

The well-to-do diners feasted on ten courses of colt-based haute cuisine prepared by a team of top chefs. They munched their way through horsemeat steaks, sausages and croquettes, all cooked with a Michelin-starred flourish. And to finish? Why, what could be more tempting than horse-foot jelly? Beside the banquet a buffet was laid on, featuring the inexpensive bits of a horse posh people wouldn't eat but the masses would obviously be happy to gobble down – brain, ears, tail, teeth, that sort of thing.

Unfortunately, one important man in the room wasn't convinced. Naturalist and foodie pioneer Frank Buckland, known for stewing anything that moved including moles, commented that the room smelled of a hard-ridden horse. His judgement was that 'hippophagy has not the slightest chance of success in this country.' Bicknell's dream was thus trampled under hoof. After all, why eat horse when you've got mole?

introducing it to his military superiors, inventing dishes such as *pot-au-feu de cheval* (a horsemeat stew) as he did so.

So it seems war has had a decisive impact on the cross-Channel divide in attitudes to horsemeat. Whereas the British create poems ('A Soldier's Kiss' by Henry Chappell), children's books (Michael Morpurgo's *War Horse*) and West End shows out of man and beast's shared experience of battle, the French create lunch.

But they weren't, and aren't, the only ones. A taste for horse also took hold in Belgium, Switzerland and Luxembourg and was exported to French Canada. Meanwhile Italians have been quietly chomping on the animal for centuries, right under the nose of the disapproving Vatican. In fact, they're so enamoured with it they're now the largest European consumers, with the meat's popularity in France declining since World War II.

In the UK it has always been a dish of last resort, never quite making the leap from a beast eaten in desperation to a bona fide part of our diet. That might be about to change.

Horse, what's it good for?

If you're looking for a red meat fix, horse is a really healthy choice. A 100g serving of horsemeat will, on average, contain around 133 calories, 5g of fat and 52mg of cholesterol. Top sirloin of beef pops up to 201 calories and 13g of fat with 47mg of cholesterol. Bacon, comparatively speaking, is a death wish in a sandwich, with 100g of cured bacon lumbering in at 458 calories, 45g of fat and 68mg of cholesterol – before you even add the bread and butter!

Perhaps it's unsurprising that horses provide the leanest of red meats, they are, after all, the health freaks of the farmyard.

You won't find them lounging around with the pigs and cows – they've got too much galloping to do. And they're picky about what they eat too. While other animals happily nosh away on whatever feed is placed before them, horses will only allow hay, oats and barley into their nosebags, occasionally nudging their heads over a fence to implore a passerby for an apple. We all deserve a treat now and again.

What's more, horses don't suffer from an array of stomach-turning conditions that afflict other animals used by the meat industry, including bird flu, mad cow disease, tuberculosis, foot-and-mouth and tapeworm. The only slight stain on its buff, disease-free reputation is bute, an anti-inflammatory drug that can trigger an adverse reaction in some humans and is illegal for use on horses destined for your dinner plate. But as long as you buy from a reputable seller there's no need to worry.

How flavoursome is this filly?

Some say a nicely-cooked hunk of horse tastes just like a good beef steak. Others compare it to venison. Either way it usually gets a positive press from people who have tried it. Among horse neigh-sayers there is a misconception that it is tough, but like most meats this is only the case if it is over-cooked. And being leaner than other red meats it needs less time in the frying pan. Since Brits have a long and proud tradition of cremation in the kitchen, this is no doubt how horse achieved its chewy reputation.

In truth, horse tends to be sweeter than beef with a gamey flavour, which is where those venison comparisons come from. The younger the beast the lighter the colour and more subtle the flavour of the meat; older animals boast a darker colour that reflects a richer flavour. And, unusually, the closer the animal is to drawing its pension, the more tender the meat.

Connoisseurs, including many of Britain's most famous chefs, prefer their meat to retain its deep red hue, which means whipping it away from the flame a couple of seconds after the horse has hit the heat. Leave it any longer and you'll be subjected to a disdainful foodie glare, and possibly violence, from the nearest grumpy French chef.

Cutting and cooking

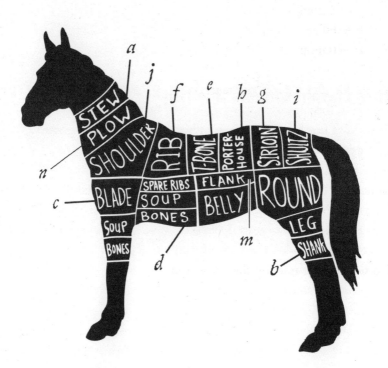

Horsemeat cuts follow the same logic as beef. This is how to use them:

Stew this for a hearty horsey hot pot:
  a – Chuck
  b – Shank
  c – Shin
  d – Skirt

Sizzle this for a stallion steak dinner:
  e – T-bone
  f – Entrecôte/rib eye
  g – Sirloin
  h – Fillet
  i – Rump

Roast this after a day at the races:
  j – Topside
  f – Entrecôte/rib eye
  g – Sirloin

Mince this for burgers, pies and bolog-neigh-se sauce:
  m – Flank
  n – Neck

Do not attempt to cook the nag's head.

Cooking times:

	Roasting	Grilling/Frying	Stewing
Temp	160°C/Gas 3	Medium heat	Medium heat on the stove or 160°C/Gas 3 in the oven
Time	10 mins/500g rare 13 mins/500g medium 15 mins/500g well done	5 mins rare 7 mins medium 10 mins well done Turn once during cooking	2 hours or until the meat is tender

The laughing horse

By now you're probably eager to start preparing a horse-themed dinner party complete with hay bales for seats, a water trough and, if you can convince him to come, Frankie Dettori.

To keep the evening trotting along nicely it would also be a good idea to arm yourself with a few relevant equine jokes, which you can drop into the conversation if it begins to sag. Pippa Middleton would undoubtedly advise you to do the same.

Keep these close to hand and your guests will leave thinking that you are both courageous in the kitchen and in possession of a wit to match playwright Oscar Wilde:

How do horses disguise themselves?
With mascarpone

What's the best way to cook horsemeat?
On the hoof

What do vegetarians use instead of horsemeat?
Uniquorn

Why could nobody hear what Dobbin was saying?
He was too horse

What did the horse say when the pig flew?
'I canter believe it'

Why did the pony cry on her wedding day?
Because the bridle suite was double booked

What put a smile on the butcher's face?
He'd found a Newmarket for horsemeat

Which band's poster is on the wall of every foal?
The Shergarbabes

How do you catch a bank-robbing horse?
Get a tip-off

A man has been rushed to hospital after trying to eat a
clothes horse.
He's in a stable condition

Why couldn't the horse buy a pint?
Because the pub didn't serve food

Why did the Shetland pony travel south?
To meet the London mare

HORSES FOR COURSES

Menu Suggestion: for Sunday lunch

Horse d'ouevres
Braised pig trotters

Mane course
Herb-crusted beef tenderloin with thoroughbred sauce

Final furlong
Golden stirrup pudding

DINING TIP

Always decanter the wine before serving

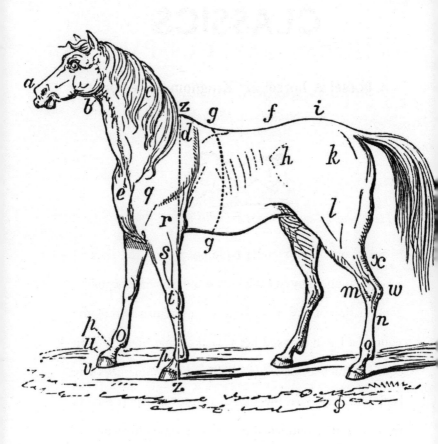

THE CLASSICS

'A horse! A horse! My Kingdom for a horse!'

Shakespeare, Richard III

In many of Europe's greatest foodie cultures the sight of a horse pounding gracefully across a meadow, a beguiling combination of power and beauty, is only surpassed by the sight of a barely-cooked horse steak sitting on a plate. In countries such as France and Italy equine dining goes way back and they have the recipes to prove it. This section focuses on the continental classics and some old favourites that can be seamlessly adapted to include a bit of nag.

Pot-au-feu de Cheval
FRENCH HORSE STEW

Made famous by the father of modern French cooking, Auguste Escoffier,
during the Franco-Prussian War of 1870-71, this is just the kind of
hearty stew an army could march for miles on. And although the French
lost this particular war, they won the best battlefield-dinner award.

SERVES 4

Ingredients:

2 cloves

1 onion, peeled

1.5kg stewing horsemeat (such as flank or neck), tied

2 garlic cloves

1 bay leaf

2.5 litres water

4 carrots, cut into chunks

2 turnips, cut into chunks

4 leeks, cut into chunks

¼ Savoy cabbage, cut into chunks

salt and freshly ground black pepper

roast potatoes, to serve

Method:

First hurdle: Push the cloves into the onion.

Second hurdle: Put the horsemeat, onion, garlic and bay leaf into a saucepan filled with 2.5 litres of salted cold water. Bring to the boil, then lower the heat to a simmer and simmer for 3 hours, skimming off any fat that rises to the surface, or until the horsemeat is tender.

Third hurdle: About an hour before the meat has finished cooking add the carrots and turnips, then after 30 minutes, add the leeks and cabbage.

Final furlong: Drain the horsemeat and vegetables, retaining the stock to serve as a gravy. Remove and discard the onion, cloves, garlic and bay leaf. Transfer the horse to a serving dish and untie the string. Carve the meat at the table and serve with a selection of the stewed vegetables, roast potatoes and horsey gravy on the side.

HORSEMEAT FACT

There are more than 700 dedicated horse butchers, *boucheries chevalines*, in France.

IF THIS DISH WAS A HORSE IT WOULD BE

A carthorse. There's nothing fancy about this robust fare. But it won't let you down.

Pastissada de Caval

VERONESE HORSE HOT POT

With thanks to Anna del Conte

'This is the name in local dialect of a dish which originated near Verona in 489 after a battle between the Italian army and the army of the invading Ostrogoths. The victorious Teodorico, king of the Ostrogoths, declared that all the horses killed in the battle should be distributed among the people and the Pastissada was born, or so the story goes.

It is a dish still very popular in the trattorie of Veneto, often made with the later addition of tomatoes and always served with polenta.'

Anna del Conte

This dish is the equivalent of a relaxing morning trot. There's no need to rush or use the whip. Marinate overnight and cook at a leisurely pace for a thoroughbred plate of food. For an extra depth of flavour pop it in the fridge after it's cooked and reheat the next day.

SERVES 6–8

Ingredients:

1kg stewing horsemeat, cut into chunks

1 bottle red wine

3–4 bay leaves

6 cloves

salt

a dozen peppercorns, crushed

50g unsalted butter

2 tbsp olive oil

3 large onions, sliced

2–3 tbsp wine vinegar

Method:

First hurdle: Put the meat in a ceramic bowl together with the wine, bay leaves, cloves, salt and peppercorns. Cover with cling film and leave to marinate in the fridge for at least 48 hours.

Second hurdle: Preheat the oven to 150°C/Gas 2.

Third hurdle: Heat the butter and oil in a large casserole and when hot throw in the onion. Sprinkle with a pinch or two of salt, cover the pot and cook gently for 20 minutes, stirring frequently. Add the meat and fry for 10 minutes or so, stirring it around in the onion. Add the marinade and bring to the boil. Put the casserole in the oven and cook for about 2 hours, stirring once or twice during the cooking.

Final furlong: Add the vinegar and put the meat back in the oven for a further half an hour. Taste and add more salt, if necessary, and some ground pepper. Serve with polenta.

IF THIS DISH WERE A HORSE IT WOULD BE
A Shire horse. Big and loveable, but not a sprinter.

Sauerbraten
GERMAN POT ROAST

*The word on the street is that Holy Roman Emperor Charlemagne
invented this creamy German classic in the 9th century as a way of
using up leftover roast meat. But let's face it, he's probably taken credit
for some lowly chef's genius. Traditionally horsemeat was this recipe's
main component, but nowadays beef is getting in on the act.
Don't follow the crowd – put a pony in the pot.*

SERVES 4

Ingredients:

750g stewing horsemeat

4 tbsp oil

2 onions, finely chopped

2 carrots, roughly chopped

2 celery sticks, roughly chopped

2 leeks, cut into large chunks

salt and freshly ground black pepper

For the marinade:

500ml white wine vinegar

500ml dry white wine

500ml water

1 tsp salt

5 black peppercorns

4 cloves

10 juniper berries

4 allspice berries

2 bay leaves

large bunch of flat-leaf parsley, finely chopped

For the sauce:

1 tbsp plain flour

125ml double cream

Method:

First hurdle: Place the marinade ingredients in a large saucepan and bring to the boil. Boil for 2 minutes, then remove from the heat and leave to cool completely.

Second hurdle: Place the horsemeat in a large earthenware bowl or pot and pour the cooled marinating liquid over it. Leave in a cool place or, in summer, in the fridge for 3 days, turning the meat every day to make sure the marinade infuses all of it.

Third hurdle: Remove the meat from the marinade, pat dry and season well with salt and pepper. Heat the oil in a large casserole over a medium to high heat. Add the meat and turn to sear and brown all over.

Fourth hurdle: Lower the heat and add the onions, carrots, celery and leeks. Allow the vegetables to colour slightly, then strain the marinade, reserving the liquid, and pour the liquid into the pot. Cover and cook on a low heat for 2–3 hours, stirring occasionally, until the meat is tender. If the marinade reduces too much, add a little more water (the sauce should be thick and rich) and check that the meat does not stick or burn. Remove the meat and transfer to a warmed serving dish.

Final furlong: To finish, make the sauce by beating the flour into the cream. Season with salt and pepper then stir into the cooking liquid and cook until thickened. Serve the horse with the sauce alongside.

Lasagne de Caval al Forno
HORSE LASAGNE

Horsemeat and lasagne have gone through some tough times recently. But as long as the relationship is in the open it really can be beautiful. The meaty tomato sauce and creamy cheese topping combine to create one of the world's great comfort foods. What's more, lasagne's ability to cater for the masses means it's a great dish with which to spread the horsey word.

SERVES 6

Ingredients:

1 tbsp olive oil

1 onion, finely chopped

1 large carrot, finely chopped

1 celery stick, finely chopped (reserve any leaves)

100g sausage meat

100g minced horsemeat

1 x 400g tin plum tomatoes

1 x 680g bottle passata

small bunch of basil

1 bay leaf

dried lasagne sheets

100g Parmesan, grated

large knob of butter

salt and freshly ground black pepper

For the béchamel sauce:

  45g butter
  3 tbsp plain flour
  600ml milk
  pinch of freshly grated nutmeg

  Preheat the oven to 200°C/Gas 6.

Method:

First hurdle: In a heavy-based saucepan or casserole, heat the olive oil over a low to medium heat and add half the vegetables. Sweat for 10–15 minutes, or until soft but not coloured. Add the sausage meat, increase the heat to medium and cook for about 5 minutes until browned, then add the horsemeat and brown all over. Add the tomatoes and passata, along with a bouquet garni of the basil tied up with the bay leaf and reserved celery leaves (remove this after cooking the sauce). Season well.

Second hurdle: Cover and simmer for about 1 hour, until the sauce looks thick and rich. Add a little water if necessary.

Third hurdle: To make the béchamel sauce, melt the butter in a small saucepan and stir in the flour, until combined. Cook, stirring, on a very low heat for a couple of minutes, then add the milk, little by little, whisking or stirring continuously to form a smooth paste. Continue to add the milk, stirring all the while. When all the milk has been added, turn up the heat and cook, stirring, until the sauce thickens. Grate in a little nutmeg, to taste, then remove from the heat and set aside.

Final furlong: Butter a lasagne or ovenproof dish, then spoon a layer of the meat sauce into the bottom of the dish. Cover with a layer of lasagne sheets, then add a thin covering of béchamel and a sprinkling of Parmesan. Continue to build the layers, finishing with a generous layer of béchamel. Dot all over with butter, then bake in the oven for 30 minutes, until bubbling and nicely browned on top. Serve immediately.

IF THIS DISH WAS A HORSE IT WOULD BE
Bullseye from *Toy Story*. A trusty friend you can rely on
in any occasion.

Stable Hand's Pie

*Move over little lamb, there's a horse in town and it's begging to be
covered in mashed potato. Give the traditional British Shepherd's Pie
an equine twist by throwing a pile of pony into the mix.*

SERVES 4

Ingredients:

900g floury potatoes (such as Desiree, King Edward or Maris
Piper), peeled and halved
2 tbsp olive oil

500g minced horsemeat
1 large onion, finely chopped
220g mushrooms, sliced
1 x 200g tin plum tomatoes
2 tbsp tomato purée
1 tsp Tabasco sauce
1 tbsp Worcestershire sauce
250ml chicken stock
120g peas (fresh or frozen)
250ml milk
30g butter
salt and freshly ground pepper, to taste

Preheat the oven to 200°C/Gas 6.

Method:

First hurdle: Place the potatoes in a pan of salted water, bring to the boil and cook for about 15 minutes, until very tender. Drain and set aside.

Second hurdle: To make the pie filling, heat the oil in a heavy-based saucepan and add the horsemeat. Cook for 4–5 minutes on a medium heat until evenly browned, stirring to make sure it doesn't stick or burn.

Third hurdle: When the meat starts to turn golden, add the onion and cook for 2 minutes, stirring. Add the mushrooms, tinned tomatoes, tomato purée, Tabasco and Worcestershire sauces and the stock. Season well and bring to the boil, then reduce the heat and simmer for 4–5 minutes. Add the peas, bring back to a simmer and cook until the peas are just tender. Remove from the heat and pour the filling into an ovenproof dish.

Fourth hurdle: Heat the milk with the butter in a small pan until very hot, but don't allow to boil. Add to the potatoes in their saucepan and mash until light and fluffy with no lumps. Season with lots of pepper and some salt. Spoon the mashed potato on top of the meat and spread with a knife to cover in an even layer, then gently score all over with a fork to make little peaks.

Final furlong: Place in the middle of the oven and cook for about 30 minutes or until the top is golden brown and crisp.

HORSEMEAT FACT

Although we Brits have never really taken to eating horsemeat, it was a popular part of the Yorkshire diet until the 1930s. As a result, Yorkshire-men were known as kicker-eaters.

IF THIS DISH WAS A HORSE IT WOULD BE

An Exmoor pony. With its double-layered coat this British breed is at its best on a cold winter's day. Just like the pie.

Braciole alla Barese
STUFFED HORSE ROLLS

Let a herd of flavours go for a gallop around your taste buds with this dish from Puglia in southern Italy. Each roll consists of horsemeat, prosciutto, cheese, parsley and garlic all bundled into a tempting meaty baton.

SERVES 4

Ingredients:

1 small onion, thinly sliced

2 garlic cloves, crushed

small bunch of flat-leaf parsley, stalks removed, finely chopped

4 x 100g fillets horsemeat, thinly sliced

80g prosciutto, thinly sliced

80g Pecorino cheese, thinly sliced

3–4 tbsp extra virgin olive oil

1 large glass dry white wine

400g passata

480ml chicken stock

1 small dried peperoncino chilli

6 basil leaves

salt and freshly ground black pepper

plain rice, to serve

Method:

First hurdle: Mix the onion, garlic and parsley together in a small bowl.

Second hurdle: Place the horse fillet slices on a chopping board, cover with a sheet of baking paper, then gently pound with a meat tenderiser or rolling pin, until thin.

Third hurdle: Prepare the rolls by covering each flattened fillet with one or two slices of prosciutto, then two slices of the cheese. Divide half the onion mix evenly between the four rolls, then roll each fillet and secure with two wooden cocktail sticks or tie with kitchen string.

Fourth hurdle: Heat the olive oil in a pan over a medium heat and add the horse rolls. Turn to brown evenly on all sides, then add the remaining onion mixture to the pan. Season well with salt and pepper, then lower the heat and cook gently for a few minutes until fragrant.

Fifth hurdle: Pour in the wine, increase the heat and bubble briskly for about 5 minutes, until the wine has reduced. Add the passata, 400ml of the stock and crumble in the peperoncino. Cover and simmer on a medium heat for 1 hour, stirring occasionally but being careful not to disturb the rolls too much. Add a little extra stock as necessary as the sauce reduces – it should be rich, dark and glossy.

Final furlong: Remove from the heat, scatter with the basil leaves and serve with plain rice.

IF THIS DISH WAS A HORSE IT WOULD BE
The Trojan horse. There's something unexpected inside.

Rôti de Cheval au Vin Rouge
GARLICKY ROAST HORSE WITH RED WINE

If horse manages to sneak into that fabled British dining tradition The Sunday Roast, it will know it has finally made it on these shores. And this could be the dish that does the trick. A succulent horse joint in garlic, onion and red wine, accompanied by potatoes, fondant or dauphinoise (okay, if that's going too far, stick with the good old roast spud) and green veg might just convert the most conservative of Sunday diners.

SERVES 4

Ingredients:

1kg lean roasting joint of horse (such as topside), tied (ask your butcher to do this)
1 large garlic clove, crushed
1 onion, finely chopped
125ml red wine
salt and freshly ground black pepper

Preheat the oven to 240°C/Gas 9.

Method:

First hurdle: Place the horse joint in a roasting dish and season well all over, then rub the garlic into the joint. Add the onion and red wine to the dish.

Second hurdle: Place the dish on the top shelf of the oven and roast for 5 minutes.

Third hurdle: Reduce the oven to 200°C/Gas 6 and continue to cook for 25–30 minutes. The roast will be rare, tender and still pink. If you like it medium, leave it in the oven for a further 5–10 minutes.

Final furlong: Serve with the juices from the roasting dish.

HORSEMEAT FACT

In 1948 Britain was rocked by a horsemeat scandal with reports suggesting two million people had eaten the meat thinking it was beef. Most of them probably wondered why their steak tasted so much better than usual.

IF THIS DISH WAS A HORSE IT WOULD BE

Gandalf's steed Shadowfax. A famous British creation touched by magic.

Rôti de Cheval a l'estragon
ROAST HORSE WITH TARRAGON

*Another twist on the trusty roast, this tasty stud of a dish finds horse
and tarragon, in the form of a delicious yoghurt and gravy sauce,
getting on indecently well.*

SERVES 4

Ingredients:

2 tbsp olive oil
1kg lean roasting joint of horse (such as topside), tied
(ask your butcher to do this)
250ml beef stock
250ml red wine
1 sachet onion gravy or soup mix
250ml natural yoghurt
medium bunch of tarragon leaves, roughly chopped
sea salt and freshly ground black pepper

Preheat the oven to 180°C/Gas 4.

Method:

First hurdle: Heat the oil in a frying pan and when hot, sear
and brown the meat on all sides. Transfer to a roasting dish.

Second hurdle: Deglaze the pan with the stock and red wine,
scraping the bottom of the pan with a wooden spoon to collect
any sticky meat residue, then add the onion gravy or soup mix.

Stir well and bring to the boil. Remove from the heat and pour over the roasting joint.

Third hurdle: Roast the meat for 30–35 minutes for medium, or more, according to how well done you like your meat. Remove the joint from the roasting dish and leave to rest for at least 5 minutes on a warmed serving dish, covered with foil.

Final furlong: Add the yoghurt and tarragon to the roasting juices and mix well. Season liberally with salt and pepper and bring to a simmer (do not allow it to boil). Serve the joint with the tarragon sauce alongside.

IF THIS DISH WAS A HORSE IT WOULD BE
A pit pony. They're used to small, dark spaces. Like an oven.

Faux Filet de Cheval in Pepper Sauce

HORSE SIRLOIN IN PEPPER SAUCE

Perhaps the only things that go together better than a horse and carriage are steak and pepper sauce. If only they rhymed. Like its beefy brethren, sirloin is one of the best cuts with a perfect balance of fat and marbling to keep the meat moist and succulent and the key to cooking steak well is to make sure your pan is searingly hot before putting the meat in. Don't have more than two steaks in the pan at once, otherwise the temperature in the pan will drop and you won't be able to maintain the blast of heat needed to colour and caramelise the outside, while keeping the inside moist and pink.

SERVES 4

Ingredients:

4 x 275g thick horse sirloin steaks
2 tbsp sunflower oil
salt and freshly ground black pepper

For the sauce:

100ml double cream
1 tsp black peppercorns, roughly crushed
2 banana shallots, finely chopped
3½ tbsp port
100ml veal or chicken stock

Method:

First hurdle: To make the sauce, heat the cream in a small pan to just before boiling. Remove from the heat and add the crushed peppercorns. Cover and leave to infuse for 30 minutes. Strain to remove the peppercorns.

Second hurdle: Meanwhile, heat the sunflower oil in a large frying pan over a high heat. Season the steaks on both sides with salt and a liberal grinding of black pepper. Add to the pan and fry over a high heat for 2 minutes each side for rare, 3–4 minutes each side for medium. Remove the steaks from the pan and set aside in a warm place.

Third hurdle: Return the pan to a low heat, add the shallots and cook until translucent. Pour in the port, increase the heat and bubble to reduce to half its volume. Add the stock and the pepper-infused cream. Cook, stirring occasionally, over a medium heat until reduced to a glossy, creamy sauce. Serve immediately.

HORSEMEAT FACT

In the Tatarstan region of Russia horsemeat is described as – 'Tartar's Viagra'.

IF THIS DISH WAS A HORSE IT WOULD BE

A sire. This is a sire-loin steak after all.

Carbonnade Flammande au Cheval
FLEMISH HORSE STEW

Forget moules and frites, it's horsemeat the Belgians really love. And they show their affection by simmering it in ale to create a deeply satisfying meal. Remember, you should never ride a horse while drinking beer but you can certainly eat one that's swimming in it.

SERVES 4

Ingredients:

2–3 tbsp olive oil
3 large onions, finely chopped
1kg horse chuck steak, cut into 2cm cubes
2 tbsp plain flour, seasoned with salt and pepper
500ml veal or light beef stock
250ml light Belgian ale
sprig of thyme
2 bay leaves
½ tbsp cider vinegar
salt and freshly ground black pepper

Method:

First hurdle: Heat 2 tablespoons of the olive oil in a large casserole pan over a medium heat and fry the onions for about 10 minutes, until golden. Remove from the pan with a slotted spoon and set aside.

Second hurdle: Add the meat to the pan in batches and brown evenly on all sides. You may need to add more oil to the pan between batches but make sure it is hot before you add more meat.

Final furlong: Add the flour to the pan and mix so that the meat is evenly coated, then cook for a few more minutes. Add the stock and stir before adding the ale, cooked onions, herbs and vinegar. Stir, cover and leave to simmer for at least 1¼ hours or until the meat is very tender and the sauce is rich and thickened.

HORSEMEAT FACT

At just over 1kg each, Belgians eat the most horsemeat per person in Europe.

IF THIS DISH WAS A HORSE IT WOULD BE

A horse from the Guinness advert. Obviously happy in the presence of beer.

Bourguignon de Cheval

There is nothing that can't be improved by spending a few hours submerged in red wine, even horsemeat, which is pretty tasty in the first place. This version of the classic beef bourguignon is a hearty crowd-pleaser that can be left to bubble away while you knock back a Bordeaux and dream of riding the winner at Aintree.

SERVES 4

Ingredients:

1kg horse braising steak, cut into large cubes

3 tbsp plain flour

25g butter

1 tbsp olive oil

100g unsmoked lardons (or chopped unsmoked streaky bacon)

2 onions, chopped

2 garlic cloves, finely chopped

2 bay leaves

1 sprig thyme

1.5 litres full bodied red wine

3 carrots, cut into thick rounds

1–2 tbsp cream or crème fraîche (optional)

salt and freshly ground black pepper

Method:

First hurdle: Toss the cubes of meat in a bowl with the flour to coat lightly. Heat the butter and oil in a large heavy-bottomed casserole pan and brown the cubed meat with the lardons.

Second hurdle: Add the chopped onions, garlic, bay leaves and thyme, then pour in the red wine. Season well and cook, covered, on a low heat for 2 hours. The sauce should not boil.

Final furlong: Add the carrots and cook for a further 30 minutes. The sauce should be rich and velvety – a little cream or crème fraîche may be added at the end of the cooking time if necessary to enrich the consistency. Remove the bay leaves before serving. Serve with a creamy potato purée.

IF THIS DISH WAS A HORSE IT WOULD BE

A Comtois. This age-old French breed is a sturdy beast that can take anything that is thrown at it. Even a bottle of red wine.

Orecchiette con Ragù di Cavalo Pugliese

PASTA WITH HORSEMEAT SAUCE

Ragù is as Italian as the Colosseum and a lot easier to eat. This version features horse and pork meat basking in a tomato and red wine jus. The sauce is then combined with orecchiette (shell-shaped pasta) to create a delightful rustic stomach stretcher.

SERVES 4

Ingredients:

3 tbsp Apulian extra virgin olive oil
1 small onion, finely chopped
1 small carrot, diced
½ celery stick, finely chopped
2 bay leaves
75g minced horsemeat
25g minced pork
1 glass red wine
450ml passata
500g orecchiette pasta
sea salt and freshly ground black pepper
grated Parmesan, to serve

Method:

First hurdle: Heat the olive oil in a frying pan on a medium to low heat. Add the onion, carrot, celery and bay leaves and sweat for 10 minutes, until softened but not coloured.

Second hurdle: Increase the heat and add the minced horsemeat and pork. Brown the meat, stirring continuously to prevent it sticking or burning, then add the red wine to deglaze the pan. Add the passata and season with salt.

Third hurdle: Turn down the heat and simmer for 1 hour. Taste and season with salt and a generous grinding of black pepper. Remove the bay leaves after cooking.

Final furlong: Cook the orecchiette according to the packet instructions. Serve with the meat sauce and grated Parmesan.

HORSEMEAT FACT

It is thought the practice of eating horse in the Italian region of Veneto established itself when Venetians supplying the Roman army with steeds couldn't resist having a nibble.

IF THIS DISH WAS A HORSE IT WOULD BE

A polydactyl horse. Legend has it that Julius Caesar used to ride one of these beasts, which boast multiple toes.

Swedish Horse Meatballs and Lingonberry Sauce

This isn't the first time horsemeat has been found in a Swedish meatball on these islands. But these ones are loud and proud about their colt-based content, and in fact the Swedes have happily dined on horsemeat for years. Best of all you don't have to go furniture shopping after eating them.

SERVES 2–3

Ingredients:

For the meatballs:

300g minced horsemeat
300g lean pork mince
1 large onion, grated
1 medium egg, beaten
3 tbsp double cream
1 tbsp dark ale
85–100g fresh breadcrumbs
1 tbsp finely chopped dill or flat-leaf parsley
plain flour, for dusting
sea salt and freshly ground black pepper
olive oil, for frying

For the sauce:

20g butter
1 tbsp plain flour
400ml fresh beef or veal stock

4 tbsp double cream
1 tbsp lemon juice
white pepper

To serve:
few sprigs of dill
lingonberry sauce (or cranberry sauce if unavailable)

Method:

First hurdle: Mix the minced horse and pork with the onion, egg, cream, ale, breadcrumbs and herbs in a large bowl. Season well. Use your hands to combine all the ingredients thoroughly. If the mixture is a little sticky, add more breadcrumbs.

Second hurdle: Using your hands, roll the mixture into walnut-sized balls. It's easier to do this with wet hands, so keep a large bowl of cold water beside you and dip your hands in as you work. Place the meatballs on a baking sheet dusted with plain flour. Lightly dust with a little more plain flour then chill for 10 minutes in the fridge.

Third hurdle: Heat a good splash of olive oil in a frying pan and fry the meatballs in batches until crisp on the outside. Remove from the pan and set aside.

Fourth hurdle: To make the sauce, add the butter to the frying pan and heat to melt. Sprinkle in the flour and whisk well to prevent lumps forming. Cook for 2 minutes, then add the stock, cream and lemon juice. Season with salt and white pepper to taste. Bring to the boil, stirring all the time, then reduce the heat and simmer until the sauce has thickened.

Final furlong: Put the meatballs back in the pan with the sauce and continue to cook until heated through. Serve scattered with the dill leaves, accompanied by the lingonberry sauce.

HORSEMEAT FACT

If you're in Sweden and come across some thinly sliced meat called hamburgerkott, that's not ham you've found it's cold cut horse.

IF THIS DISH WAS A HORSE IT WOULD BE

A Dala horse, the traditional carved and painted wooden horse from the Swedish province of Dalarna. These days you can probably build one from a flat pack.

HORSES FOR COURSES

Menu Suggestion: for romance

Horse d'ouevres

*Asparagus, mozzarella and prosciutto
with an olive oil dressage*

Mane course

Steak and oyster piebald

Final furlong

Poached pears with Red Rum

DINING TIP

Remember everybody likes a dash of confidence
in their date so don't be shire

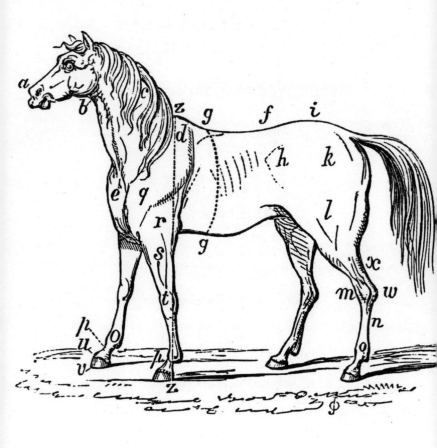

HORSING AROUND THE WORLD

'A canter is a cure for every evil.'

Benjamin Disraeli

A dash of the exotic can do wonders for a relationship even it's the one you're having with horsemeat. After all you don't want to get stuck in a rut, recycling the same old recipes each evening before arguing about the washing up. Again. Instead show your favourite cut of colt a good time by taking it on a journey around the world. Then eat it.

Chilli con Carne de Caballo

Chilli fuelled the cowboy pioneers of the Wild West. And you'll feel like you're breaking new ground in the kitchen by swapping horse for beef in this much-loved dish. Just don't cook the animal you're supposed to be riding home on.

SERVES 4

Ingredients:

1 tbsp olive oil

1 onion, finely chopped

2 garlic cloves, finely chopped

2 tsp chilli powder, or more, to taste

½ tsp dried thyme

1 tsp ground cumin

450g horse fillet, cut into fine strips

200g mushrooms, chopped

1 x 400g tin chopped tomatoes

2 tbsp tomato purée

1 tbsp Worcestershire sauce

150–200ml beef stock

Tabasco sauce, to taste

1 bay leaf

1 x 400g tin red kidney beans, drained and rinsed

salt and freshly ground black pepper

plain rice, to serve

soured cream, to serve

Method:

First hurdle: Heat the oil in a heavy-based pan over a medium heat and fry the onion and garlic gently for 4–5 minutes or until soft and lightly golden. Add the chilli powder, thyme and cumin and cook gently for 2 minutes, until fragrant.

Second hurdle: Add the strips of horsemeat and cook for 5–6 minutes until browned all over. Add all the remaining ingredients, except the kidney beans, adding only 150ml of the beef stock to begin with. Bring to a simmer, then reduce the heat, stir and cover. Leave to simmer on a low heat for 5–10 minutes.

Final furlong: Once the meat is tender, add the red kidney beans and reheat gently. Remove and discard the bay leaf. Serve with rice and a dollop of soured cream.

IF THIS DISH WAS A HORSE IT WOULD BE
Silver. Just like the Lone Ranger's trusty steed, *chilli con carne de caballo* can be relied upon to keep you alive in the Texan desert.

Horsemeat Fajitas

Give your taste buds the ride of their life by dousing sizzled stallion in hot salsa before wrapping it all in a handy-to-hold tortilla.

SERVES 4

Ingredients:

2 tbsp sunflower oil
1 red onion, finely sliced
½ red pepper, sliced
½ green pepper, sliced
125ml ready-made hot salsa sauce
450g horse sirloin, cut into strips
salt and freshly ground black pepper

To serve:

4 corn tortillas
soured cream
coriander sprigs

Preheat the oven to 200°C/Gas 6.

Method:

First hurdle: Heat the sunflower oil in a frying pan set over a high heat and fry the vegetables until cooked but still retaining a bit of crunch. Add the salsa and heat through; then remove from the pan, transfer to an ovenproof dish and place in the oven to keep warm.

Second hurdle: Return the frying pan to a high heat, then add the horsemeat strips and sear quickly – they should be cooked rare. Mix the meat with the vegetables and salsa, then check the seasoning.

Final furlong: To serve, gently warm the tortillas in the oven. Fill each tortilla with the horsemeat mixture, add a dollop of soured cream and a couple of coriander sprigs. Fold up and serve.

HORSEMEAT FACT

Che Guevara ate horsemeat when fighting in the Cuban Revolutionary War.

IF THIS DISH WAS A HORSE IT WOULD BE

An Azteca. Born and bred in Mexico.

Spicy Mexican Fricassee

Prove you're a horse-eating hard man by dropping an extra jalapony pepper into this spicy central American stew. It takes under half-an-hour to get it from stable to table. All you need to add is some warm some tortillas and an appetite for horse.

SERVES 4

Ingredients:

1 tbsp sunflower oil

450g minced horsemeat

1 onion, chopped

1 red pepper, diced

2 garlic cloves, crushed

2 tsp ground cumin

4 tsp chilli powder

½ tbsp finely chopped jalapeño pepper

2 x 400g tins chopped tomatoes, drained of their juice

1 tbsp tomato purée

125g sweetcorn (tinned or frozen)

125ml beef stock

1 x 400g tin kidney beans, drained and rinsed

salt and freshly ground black pepper

To serve:

plain rice or warm tortillas

bunch of fresh coriander, chopped

150g Cheddar, grated

soured cream

Method:

First hurdle: Heat the oil in a saucepan over a high heat and brown the meat quickly. Reduce the heat, add the onion, red pepper and garlic and sweat for 5 minutes, until softened. Add the cumin, chilli powder, jalapeño, drained tomatoes, tomato purée, sweetcorn and stock.

Second hurdle: Bring to the boil then reduce the heat and leave to bubble away, uncovered, for 15 minutes or until the sauce is reduced and thickened. Add the kidney beans, season with salt and pepper and cook for a few minutes to heat the beans through.

Final furlong: Serve in warmed bowls with rice or tortillas. Sprinkle with fresh coriander and the Cheddar and add a good dollop of soured cream.

IF THIS DISH WAS A HORSE IT WOULD BE
A hot-blooded Arabian, it's a fiery breed.

Beshbarmak
KAZAKHSTANI HORSE ON NOODLES

Nibble your way through a bowl of fingers. Five fingers to be precise,
which is the literal translation of 'beshbarmak', Kazakhstan's national
dish. Don't worry, there aren't actually any digits involved but, according
to tradition, you should really eat this horse, lamb and Kazakh horse
sausage meat-fest with your bare hands. If you can't find any sujuk or
kazy Kazakh sausage you can always pop in some pepperoni instead.
And if you have time, leave the meat to marinate overnight.

SERVES 6

Ingredients:
500g horse rump
500g lamb shank, on the bone
2 bay leaves

For the marinade:
3 garlic cloves, crushed
4 tsp sea salt
freshly ground black pepper

For the sauce:
1 tbsp vegetable oil
2 large onions, sliced into rings

For the fresh noodles:
300g plain flour
½ tsp salt
1 egg

(Ready-made dried noodles called *zhaima* can be used instead, if available. You might find them in Russian or Polish delis. Or use dried lasagne sheets.)

To serve:

2 potatoes, peeled
2 carrots, peeled
vegetable oil
1 whole *sujuk* or *kazy* sausage (optional)
small bunch of flat-leaf parsley, chopped
small bunch of chives, chopped
small bunch of dill, chopped

Method:

First hurdle: Start by marinating the meat, ideally the day before but at least 2–3 hours before cooking. Put the horse rump and lamb in a large freezer bag, add the garlic, salt and pepper and rub all over the meat, then place in the fridge.

Second hurdle: When you are ready to start cooking, place the meat in a large saucepan, just cover with cold water and bring to the boil.

Third hurdle: Drain, rinse the meat and return to the saucepan. Add cold water to just cover again and bring to the boil. Add the bay leaves. Remove any surface scum with a slotted spoon, then cover and leave to simmer for 2–2½ hours, adding more water if necessary to keep the cooking liquid level with the meat.

Fourth hurdle: Remove from the heat and leave to cool in the broth for 1–2 hours, after which transfer the meat to a separate dish (reserving the stock), cover and set aside until serving.

Fifth hurdle: To prepare the flat noodles, sift the flour into a bowl and stir in the salt. Make a well in the middle and crack in the egg, then add 100ml of the reserved cooled stock. Mix, first with a metal spoon, then with your hands, working the dough until it is smooth. The dough should be soft and workable. If it is too dry, add more stock (1 or 2 tablespoons) and work in again with your hands. Form the dough into a ball, wrap in cling film and leave to rest at room temperature for 30 minutes.

Sixth hurdle: To make the noodles, divide the dough into three equal pieces. Take a piece at a time and roll out as thinly as possible (about 2–3mm thick) on a well-floured surface. You may need to flour the rolling pin too to prevent the dough from sticking. Cut the dough into rectangles roughly 5cm x 8cm. Leave the noodles to dry on a floured surface for 30 minutes before cooking.

Seventh hurdle: Prepare the onion sauce. Take 600ml of the cooking stock and place in a small saucepan. Cook on a medium heat, uncovered, for 15 minutes or until it is reduced by half. In a separate pan, heat the vegetable oil, then add the onions and sweat over a low to medium heat until translucent. Season well, then add the reduced meat stock. Remove from the heat, cover and leave to rest for 30 minutes.

Eighth hurdle: Bring the remaining cooking stock back to the boil, then add the potatoes and carrots and cook for 20 minutes. Remove with a slotted spoon, transfer to a plate and keep warm.

Ninth hurdle: Now add the noodles to the simmering meat stock and cook for 3–4 minutes (or according to the packet instructions if using shop-bought noodles). Drain into a separate pan to retain the cooking broth, then keep the broth warm over a low heat until ready to serve.

Tenth hurdle: Reheat the onion sauce.

Eleventh hurdle: To serve, brush a warmed shallow serving dish with a little vegetable oil. Arrange the noodles and slices of horse sausage (if using) in the dish. Slice the horse rump and lamb and place on top of the noodles along with the potatoes and carrots cut into slices. Cover with the hot onion sauce and sprinkle with most of the parsley, chives and dill.

Final furlong: Serve the hot meat broth in separate bowls sprinkled with more chopped fresh herbs.

HORSEMEAT FACT

During the 2012 London Olympics the Kazakhstan team brought its own supply of kazy horsemeat sausages to fuel its weightlifters and wrestlers. It worked – they won 4 gold and 3 bronze medals respectively.

IF THIS WAS A HORSE IT WOULD BE:

The Kazakh of course. A hardy breed and obviously no stranger to the cooking pot.

Yuk Hui

KOREAN RAW HORSE SALAD
WITH GARLIC AND PINE NUTS

If horses could talk they would tell you this is how they'd want to be eaten. Fresh from the field, unadulterated by a flame and using the leanest strips of meat – just how nature intended it. Mobile phones, horsemeat . . . is there nothing the Koreans can't master?

Asian supermarkets will stock nashi pears, but if you can't get hold of them, simply substitute a firm pear, such as a Comice or Williams.

SERVES 2–3 AS A STARTER

Ingredients:

200g horse sirloin or fillet

2 garlic cloves, very finely sliced

1 tbsp pine nuts, toasted

1 nashi pear (Asian pear), cut into very fine strips (ideally using a mandoline)

1 tsp lemon juice

6 iceberg lettuce leaves

For the sauce:

2 tsp paprika

2 tbsp caster sugar

2 tsp sesame oil

1½ tbsp light soy sauce

½ garlic clove, crushed

½ tsp freshly ground black pepper

2 tsp toasted sesame seeds

Method:

First hurdle: Wrap the horsemeat in cling film and place in the freezer for 20 minutes.

Second hurdle: Place all the sauce ingredients in a bowl and mix well with a fork to combine.

Third hurdle: Remove the meat from the freezer and slice into thin strips. Add to the sauce along with the garlic and toasted pine nuts. Leave to marinate for about 15 minutes.

Final furlong: Arrange the pear on individual plates and sprinkle with the lemon juice. Spoon the marinated horse steak on top, with the lettuce leaves around the side. Serve immediately.

HORSEMEAT FACT

The lengthy life expectancy enjoyed by people living in Nagano Prefecture in Japan has been attributed to their taste for raw horsemeat.

IF THIS DISH WAS A HORSE IT WOULD BE

Champion sprinter Frankel. Lean and finished before you know it.

Laham taz-Ziemel
MALTESE STALLION IN WINE SAUCE

*The Mediterranean island of Malta has been embroiled in a
love-affair with the horse for years. Its people race and ride the
beast with gusto but appreciate it most when it has spent a
few hours soaking in red wine.*

SERVES 4

Ingredients:

500g stewing horsemeat, cubed
200ml red wine
1 tbsp olive oil
1 onion, sliced
1 garlic clove, crushed
small bunch of basil leaves
2 tsp marjoram, finely chopped (or 1 tsp dried marjoram)
½ tsp paprika
zest of ¼ lemon
zest of ¼ orange
1 tbsp tomato purée
salt
freshy crusty bread, to serve

Method:

First hurdle: Sprinkle the meat with salt, place in a bowl and
pour over the red wine. Leave to marinate for a couple of hours.

Second hurdle: Heat the olive oil in a heavy-based casserole pan over a medium heat, then gently fry the onion and garlic until translucent. Add the herbs, spices, lemon and orange zest and gently fry for a few minutes, until fragrant.

Final furlong: Add the meat and its marinade to the pan and stir in the tomato purée. Cover and cook on a low heat for 1–2 hours or until the meat is very tender. Serve with plenty of fresh bread to soak up the rich sauce.

HORSEMEAT FACT

If you're feeling a little anaemic eat horsemeat; it has twice the amount of vitamin B12 than beef.

IF THIS DISH WAS A HORSE IT WOULD BE

A trotter. Used to dragging a two-wheeled cart around Malta's race course, this beast can also carry plenty of zesty flavours.

Arrosto di Puledro
ROAST FOAL WITH CURRY

Gently fizzle your taste buds with a mild curry designed to complement the subtle flavour of young horsemeat. This foal's paradise isn't a dish you'll find on any of the takeway menus in your kitchen drawer.

SERVES 4–6

Ingredients:

2 tbsp olive oil

50g butter

1 garlic clove, very finely sliced

1 tbsp rosemary leaves

800g–1kg foal roasting joint

1 tsp mild curry powder

120ml white wine or brandy

300ml vegetable stock, heated

½ tbsp plain flour

240ml milk

salt and freshly ground black pepper

Preheat the oven to 180°C/Gas 4.

Method:

First hurdle: Heat the olive oil and butter in a roasting tin set over a medium heat and add the garlic and rosemary. Add the foal joint to the pan and sprinkle with the curry powder. Brown the joint all over, then season with salt and pepper and pour the wine over the meat.

Second hurdle: Cover the roasting tin loosely with foil and roast in the oven for 1½–2 hours, basting occasionally with the heated stock.

Third hurdle: When tender, remove the joint from the roasting dish and set aside to rest for 10 minutes.

Final furlong: To make a gravy, place the roasting tin with its juices over a medium heat. Mix the flour with the milk in a cup, making sure there are no lumps, then stir into the pan juices. Continue to stir until the gravy thickens.

HORSEMEAT FACT

Foal is considered a delicacy in Iceland along with puffin, whale and fermented shark. And people have a problem with horsemeat ...

IF THIS DISH WAS A HORSE IT WOULD BE

Yeats. The Irish stallion was a tasty bet from a young age, winning his first race aged two before going on to triumph four years in a row in the Ascot Gold Cup.

Airag
MONGOLIAN FERMENTED HORSE MILK

*Let's face it, most of you probably don't have a horse on hand to milk.
But if you ever find yourself living on the Mongolian steppe and in
desperate need of a splash of the white stuff, well you'll be thanking the
lord you've read this book. Airag is horse-loving Mongolia's national
drink and unlike the milk in your cappuccino it's slightly fizzy and a
bit boozy, containing around 2% alcohol.*

Method:

First hurdle: Milk your mare.

Second hurdle: Filter the milk through a cloth and pour
into a large open leather bag called a khukhuur. You could also
use a larch wood vat called a gan, or, in the unlikely event you
don't own either, you can use a plastic container. Hang it at the
entrance of your yurt.

Third hurdle: Leave the milk for a couple of days so that
fermentation, due to the reaction of lactic acid bacteria and
yeast, can occur. To make sure your milk ferments equally,
regularly stir it with a wooden Mongolian implement called a
buluur. Or just use a spoon. Traditionally everybody leaving or
entering your yurt should give the airag a little punch.

Fourth hurdle: Pour the airag into a bowl and offer it
to visitors. Mongolians will gulp down the whole lot, but
it's perfectly acceptable to take a small sip and return the

bowl. Refusing it completely though is considered rude and ungracious. If you're squeamish, just shut your eyes and think of a latte.

Final furlong: If you fancy a milk-based drinking session, distil your airag to make Mongol Arkhi, a stronger milk liquor.

HORSE-MILK FACT

If you drink it straight from the udder, untreated, horse milk is a powerful laxative. Which is the last thing you want when the nearest toilet is a hole in the ground.

IF THIS DISH WAS A HORSE IT WOULD BE

A unicorn. White and unlikely to cross your path.

Fondue Bourguignonne with Aïoli
SWISS HORSE FONDUE

*This is the only activity you should undertake with a horse near a
vat of hot cooking oil. Gather your friends and plunge raw steak into
the simmering liquid then cool it off in an aïoli made the traditional
way with a mortar and pestle. Or just blitz the ingredients in a food
processor. Either way the key to a successful aïoli is to make sure all
your ingredients and implements are at room temperature.*

SERVES 3–4

Ingredients:

200–250g horse fillet per person, cut into 5cm cubes
vegetable, rapeseed or sunflower oil

For the aïoli sauce:

4 garlic cloves, very finely chopped
pinch of sea salt
1 tsp Dijon mustard
2 egg yolks
120ml extra virgin olive oil
½ tsp water
1 tsp lemon juice

Method:

First hurdle: For the aïoli, put the garlic and salt in the mortar
bowl and grind slowly. In a separate metal bowl, whisk the
mustard, then add the egg yolks and continue to whisk.

Second hurdle: Slowly pour in half the oil, in a fine steady stream, whisking all the while. The sauce should start to emulsify and thicken as you whisk. Again, slowly add the water and the lemon juice, whisking continuously. Add the rest of the oil slowly and in a steady stream – the aïoli will thicken as you keep whisking. The consistency should be slightly looser than shop-bought mayonnaise.

Third hurdle: Once thickened, add the pounded garlic and salt mixture. Set aside at room temperature until ready to serve.

Final furlong: For the fondue, heat the oil in a fondue pot or earthenware casserole and place in the centre of the dining table. Once hot, guests should help themselves to morsels of meat using a fondue fork and plunge them into the hot oil until just cooked but still pink.

HORSEMEAT FACT

On average the Swiss eat between 600g and 700g of horsemeat each a year.

IF THIS DISH WAS A HORSE IT WOULD BE

A Friesian. This breed just loves going for a dip.

Shabu Shabu

JAPANESE BEEF-BROTH HORSE FONDUE

The Swiss aren't the only ones who enjoy communal cooking, the Japanese are partial to a spot of table-top cheffery too. This healthy version of the traditional fondue has diners boiling their horsemeat chunks in a fragrant beef broth rather than oil.

SERVES 4

Ingredients:

400g horse fillet

100g spring onions, sliced lengthways into thin strips

100g baby carrots, sliced lengthways into thin strips

125g pak choi, quartered through the centre

100g spinach

100g shiitake mushrooms, wiped clean

100g enoki mushrooms, wiped clean

250g Japanese noodles (udon or similar)

2 tsp sesame oil

500ml fresh beef stock

1 tsp light soy sauce

1 tsp grated fresh ginger

For the ponzu dipping sauce:

4 tbsp rice vinegar

2 tbsp mirin (rice wine)

3 tbsp light soy sauce

1½ tbsp fresh lemon juice

Accompaniments:
  wasabi
  Japanese pickled vegetables
  Japanese pickled ginger
  soy sauce
  ponzu dipping sauce

Method:

First hurdle: Wrap the horsemeat fillet in cling film and place in the freezer for about 20 minutes. This helps when slicing it thinly.

Second hurdle: Arrange the vegetables on a serving plate and set aside.

Third hurdle: Make the ponzu dipping sauce by mixing all the ingredients together in a small bowl, then set aside.

Fourth hurdle: Cook your noodles according to the packet instructions, then drain and rinse. Transfer to a serving bowl, add the sesame oil and toss to mix.

Fifth hurdle: Slice the horsemeat into 1cm-wide strips and arrange on a serving plate.

Sixth hurdle: To make your broth, bring the stock to the boil with the soy sauce and ginger in a fondue pot in the centre of the table. Add the vegetables to the stock – carrots first as they take longer to cook. When tender, guests should help themselves to morsels of meat and, using a fondue fork, dip briefly in the broth until cooked but still pink.

Final furlong: Once all the meat and vegetables are finished, add the noodles to the broth then divide among your guests and serve with the ponzu dipping sauce and other accompaniments.

HORSEMEAT FACT

The Japanese for horsemeat is 'baniku', but they also refer to it as 'sakura-niku' which translates as 'cherry meat'. This is how you should describe it if any reticent diners are coming over.

IF THIS DISH WAS A HORSE IT WOULD BE

A stock horse. If there's any horse that wouldn't mind mixing with a bit of beef broth it's this one, boasting an excellent working relationship with cattle it is said to have 'cow sense'.

Paardenlapjes in Aromatische Saus
HORSE FILLET IN AROMATIC SAUCE

When William of Orange invaded England in 1688 he brought around 4,000 cavalrymen with him, so this isn't the first time a horse from Holland has made an impression on these islands. In this Dutch dish the sweet flavour of horsemeat is complemented by a herby tomato sauce that might just cause a Glorious Revolution in your mouth.

SERVES 4

Ingredients:

- 4 tbsp olive oil
- 4 x 120g lean horse fillet steaks
- 1 onion, sliced
- 100g pancetta, diced
- 200ml red wine
- 1 x 200g tin chopped tomatoes
- small bunch of flat-leaf parsley, finely chopped
- sprig of rosemary, finely chopped
- salt and freshly ground black pepper

Method:

First hurdle: Heat the oil in a non-stick frying pan over a high heat. Flash-fry the horse steaks for about 30 seconds on each side, to seal the meat. Remove the fillets from the pan and set aside.

Second hurdle: Add the onion and pancetta to the frying pan and cook on a medium heat for about 4 minutes, until the onion is soft and the pancetta sizzling.

Final furlong: Pour the red wine into the pan and cook until it has reduced by half. Add the tomatoes and their liquid and stir. Simmer for 3–5 minutes then add the horse steaks, along with the herbs and salt and pepper to taste, and continue to cook for 3 minutes in the sauce on a medium heat, turning the steaks once, until cooked to your liking.

HORSEMEAT FACT

Holland's famous frikandel sausage is often made with horsemeat. By the by, the world record for the most frikandellen eaten in an hour is 47.

IF THIS DISH WAS A HORSE IT WOULD BE

King William's favourite steed, Sorrel. A beast clearly capable of carrying something auspicious from the Netherlands.

Battered Chinese Crispy Shredded Horse

The Chinese are enthusiastic consumers of horse and this take on a classic oriental dish is one very good reason why.

SERVES 4 AS A STARTER

Ingredients:

3 heaped tbsp cornflour, plus extra for dusting

1 level tsp table salt

3 eggs

300g horse fillet steak, cut into thin strips about 7mm wide and 5–6cm long

vegetable oil, for frying

plain rice, to serve

For the sauce:

2 carrots, shredded

2–3 spring onions, shredded

1 large garlic clove, crushed

3cm knob of fresh ginger, peeled and cut into very fine strips

2 red chillies, cut into very fine strips

20g caster sugar

4 tbsp rice wine vinegar

4 tbsp sweet chilli sauce

1 tbsp light soy sauce

Method:

First hurdle: Pour some vegetable oil into a wok or deep frying pan to a depth of about 1cm.

Second hurdle: Combine the cornflour and salt in a mixing bowl, make a well in the middle and add the eggs one by one, whisking well to form a smooth batter with no lumps.

Third hurdle: Heat the oil. To test if it's hot enough, drop in a little batter. It should sizzle and turn golden when the oil is the correct temperature.

Fourth hurdle: Lightly coat the horse strips in cornflour, then dip the strips in the batter, shaking them to remove any excess. Add them one by one to the wok. Allow them to sizzle for about 10 seconds before stirring so that they don't stick in clumps (you may need to fry the strips in batches). Fry over a high heat until the batter has turned deep golden brown and is crisp. Remove with a slotted spoon onto some kitchen paper to drain. Keep warm.

Final furlong: In a separate pan or wok, heat a little of the cooking oil, then stir-fry the shredded carrot with the spring onions, garlic, chilli and ginger for about a minute. Add the sugar, then the rest of the ingredients and stir-fry for a couple of minutes or until the sauce has thickened and is slightly sticky. Finally, add the fried horse strips and stir briefly to coat with the sticky chilli sauce. Serve with plain rice.

Horsemeat dishes are particularly popular in the southern
Chinese region of Guangxi.

IF THIS DISH WAS A HORSE IT WOULD BE

A Guoxia. This Chinese pony is small but perfectly formed.
Like this starter.

Horse Steak Tartare Japanese-style

*Whisper this in France, but the French aren't the only ones who know
how to whip up a decent tartare. The Japanese are experienced raw horse
handlers and have given the delicacy an eastern twang.*

*With many thanks for this recipe to Gillan Kingstree – head chef at
Oliver Peyton's National Dining Rooms*

SERVES 3–4 AS A STARTER

Ingredients:

200g best rump of horse, julienned (cut into short thin strips)
100g daikon radish, julienned
50ml tonkatsu sauce
25g coriander, chopped
75g goma-ae (sesame) dressing
salt and pepper, to taste

To garnish:

black radish, cut into thin strips

3–4 egg yolks

Method:

First hurdle: Mix all the ingredients together in a bowl and arrange to form a circle on each plate, using a pastry ring as a guide.

Final furlong: Garnish with strips of black radish and top each dish with an egg yolk. Serve immediately.

HORSEMEAT FACT

Raw horsemeat is full of cholesterol-bashing linoleic acid.

IF THIS DISH WAS A HORSE IT WOULD BE

Joie De Vivre. A Japanese racehorse with a French name.

Horsemeat Stroganoff

Russians are old hands when it comes to equine dining. Moscow's restaurants serve it, the nation's nomadic tribes survive on it and you'll love it in this Russian classic.

SERVES 4

Ingredients:

30g butter
1 tbsp olive oil
2 onions, thinly sliced
500g horse fillet, cut into thin slices, about 1cm x 4cm
250g button mushrooms, cleaned and sliced
2 tbsp brandy
juice of ½ lemon
250ml soured cream
1 tbsp paprika, or to taste
sea salt and freshly ground black pepper
finely chopped flat-leaf parsley, to garnish
boiled rice, tagliatelle or other fresh noodles, to serve

Method:

First hurdle: Heat half the butter and the oil in a frying pan and sweat the onions until translucent and just beginning to turn golden. Add the meat, mushrooms and the rest of the butter and brown for about 4 minutes.

Second hurdle: Add the brandy, and cook on a medium heat until reduced. Mix the lemon juice with the soured cream and paprika, then add to the pan. Season and bring to the boil. Remove from the heat and sprinkle the stroganoff with finely chopped parsley and a little extra paprika, if liked.

Final furlong: Serve with rice, tagliatelle or noodles.

HORSEMEAT FACT

Some Russian stores sell canned horsemeat.

IF THIS DISH WAS A HORSE IT WOULD BE

A Russian Don. When it comes to Russian horsemeat cuisine this dish is the don.

HORSES FOR COURSES

Menu Suggestion: for spice

Horse d'ouevres

Masala spiced nag paneer

Mane course

Free rein-ge chicken vindaloo

Final furlong

Chilli and chocolate Desert Orchid dusted in icing Shergar

DINING TIP

You'd be a foal not to have a glass of water handy

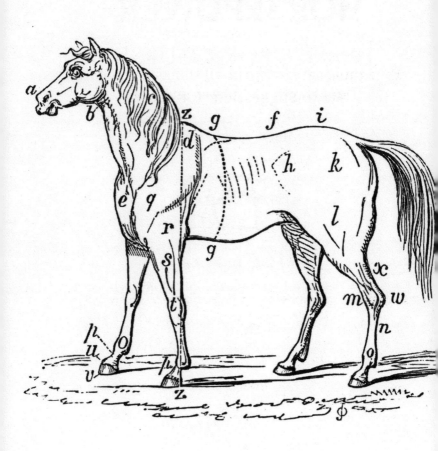

HORSEPOWER

'Four things greater than all things are women
and horses and power and war.'

Rudyard Kipling

Certain occasions demand hulking hunks of red meat.
Often these occasions involve men standing around talking
about sport. Such moments call for the largest steaks,
burgers and sausages you can lay your hands on, all cluttered
under the grill or on a barbecue in a sizzling monument
to man's love of meat. Surely nobody will mind if some of
it comes from a horse?

Horse Burgers with Cheese

Your average shop-bought burger is 50% dust, 30% reconstituted iguana and 20% beef flavouring. Or something similar. If you want to be utterly sure of what you're eating, it's best to break out the horse mince and make your own burger patties.

SERVES 4

Ingredients:

600g minced horsemeat

2 banana shallots, finely chopped

2 eggs

1 tbsp dried mixed herbs (tarragon, basil, thyme)

2 tbsp finely chopped flat-leaf parsley

2 tbsp olive oil (optional, if frying the burgers)

To serve:

4 burger buns

4 slices Emmental or other hard cheese

1 tomato, sliced

1 small red onion, cut into rings

Tapenade, salsa, relishes or mustard

Preheat your oven grill to high (or low if you're frying your burgers).

Method:

First hurdle: In a bowl, use your hands to mix the minced meat, shallots, eggs and herbs together well, then divide the mixture into four evenly-sized patties, about 1–2cm thick.

Second hurdle: You can either grill or fry the patties. To grill, place them under the hot grill for 5–6 minutes each side. To fry, heat the olive oil in a frying pan over a medium to high heat. Fry for 7–8 minutes each side.

Third hurdle: Grill or toast your burger buns. When the burgers are ready, turn the grill down to low and layer each burger with a slice of cheese, then place under the grill and cook until the cheese is just melting.

Final furlong: Serve the cheesy horse burgers in their buns, with a slice of tomato and some onion rings, and your preferred condiments.

HORSEMEAT FACT

When meat was scarce in the US during World War II many Americans went looking for their fix in the stable. Republicans blamed President Truman for this turn of events and nicknamed him Horsemeat Harry.

IF THIS DISH WAS A HORSE IT WOULD BE
A ranch horse. An old American favourite.

Tournedos de Cheval

A tournedos is a small, round, thick steak cut from the horse's tenderloin. The secret to getting the best out of it is to do very little. Cook on a high heat and not for too long unless you want to experience what it might be like to chew on an old saddle. Otherwise, this dainty, flavour-filled cut needs only a simple gravy to help it along. Accompany it with some mash or thick-cut chips or, if you're having a Gallic moment, garlicky sautéed potatoes or thin-cut fries, for a ridiculously satisfying feast.

SERVES 4

Ingredients:

1 tbsp finely chopped flat-leaf parsley

1 tbsp finely chopped tarragon

2 garlic cloves, crushed

2 tbsp olive oil

4 x 180g tournedos horse steaks

200ml beef stock

sea salt and freshly ground black pepper

Method:

First hurdle: Mix the herbs, garlic and oil in a cup. Brush the steaks on each side with the seasoned oil.

Second hurdle: Place a heavy-based non-stick frying pan over a very high heat. When hot, place the steaks in the pan and cook for about 4 minutes each side or until done to your liking. Remove from the pan and keep warm.

Final Furlong: Deglaze the pan with the stock, scraping the bottom with a wooden spoon to remove any sticky residue, then bring to the boil and leave to bubble and reduce until thickened slightly. Season to taste, and serve each tournedos with a little of the reduced stock.

HORSEMEAT FACT

Horsemeat is a rich source of iron – beef has less than half the content.

IF THIS DISH WAS A HORSE IF WOULD BE:

A Yukutian. This Siberian breed is used to the cold and doesn't appreciate being subjected to too much heat.

Horsemeat Sirloin Steaks
with Plum Sauce

Give a man a sirloin steak and he'll be your friend for life,
give him one with a plum sauce and he'll marry you.
Or at least he'll ask you for the recipe.

SERVES 4

Ingredients:

4 tbsp extra virgin olive oil
1 shallot, finely chopped
4 tbsp white wine
125g plums, halved
2 tsp white wine vinegar
1 tsp maple syrup
4 tbsp rich beef stock
dash of Madeira
4 x 275g horse sirloin steaks
dressed green salad, to serve

Method:

First hurdle: Heat half the olive oil in a frying pan over a
low to medium heat and sweat the shallots until soft but not
coloured. Add the white wine and simmer to reduce to half its
volume. Add the plums and simmer for a couple of minutes,
then add the vinegar, maple syrup and beef stock along with a
dash of Madeira. Simmer for 1 minute, then set aside.

Second hurdle: Heat the remaining oil in a separate frying pan over a very high heat. Once hot, fry the steaks for 2–4 minutes on each side (depending on how well done you like your horsemeat; see the cooking time chart on page 12).

Final furlong: Serve with the sauce and a crisp green salad.

HORSEMEAT FACT

It is believed Mongolian horsemen used to tenderise their steaks by riding with them wedged under their saddles.

IF THIS DISH WAS A HORSE IT WOULD BE

A medicine horse. Plums are heralded as the new super-food by scientists due to their high levels of antioxidants and phytonutrients.

Marinated Horse Kebabs

Britain loves a kebab. Usually it comes in one of two forms: skewered chunks of marinated juicy flesh sizzled on the barbecue or a pita full of unidentified meat shavings eaten after ten pints and a scuffle with a bouncer. This recipe is the former. Simple and delicious.

SERVES 4

Ingredients:

500g topside of horse, cut into large cubes
2 red peppers, deseeded and diced
small bunch of chives, to garnish
sesame seeds, to garnish

For the marinade:

5 tbsp mirin (rice wine) or rice vinegar
5 tbsp soy sauce
5 tbsp sake
1 tsp sugar

barbecue skewers

Method:

First hurdle: Prepare the marinade. Mix all the ingredients together in a large bowl. Add the meat to the marinade and mix to ensure all the pieces are coated. Place in the fridge to marinate for several hours.

Second hurdle: Thread the meat on to the skewers with a square of pepper between each piece. Pour the reserved marinade into a saucepan and simmer until reduced to a fairly thick sticky sauce.

Final furlong: Place the horse kebabs on the barbecue or under a hot grill for 4–5 minutes, turning to cook on each side. When done, sprinkle with chives and sesame seeds and serve with the sticky sauce.

IF THIS DISH WAS A HORSE IT WOULD BE

A hobby horse. Just like an equine kebab it's a stallion on a stick.

Barbecued Topside of Horse with Baby Vegetables and Pink Garlic Sauce

Another one to fire up the charcoal for, this dish brings together the yin and yang of the countryside in spring. Imagine a scene involving a mighty stallion galloping through a meadow blooming with dainty young flowers. Then imagine that on a plate, a mix of strong meaty flavours, light crunchy baby vegetables and tangy garlic. If you can, use Lautrec garlic for the sauce. Hailing from southern France and harvested in June or July, it is sold as 'fresh garlic'. If you can't get hold of it, just use standard garlic, but it's worth seeking out – it will give the sauce a much greater depth of flavour.

SERVES 4

Ingredients:

8 new-season carrots with their tops

4 baby turnips

1 tbsp olive oil

8 Jersey new potatoes, scrubbed and halved lengthways

1 tsp finely chopped thyme

2 x 200g pieces topside of horse, cut in half

8 baby onions, peeled

1 courgette, cut lengthways into thin slices

2 pink garlic cloves (Lautrec garlic), finely chopped

4–5 tbsp double cream

sea salt and freshly ground black pepper

Method:

First hurdle: Cook the new carrots and turnips in boiling salted water for 5 minutes. Drain and plunge into cold water, then set aside.

Second hurdle: Place a frying pan with about a teaspoon of the olive oil over a medium heat, add the potatoes and sprinkle with the chopped thyme. Season well with salt and pepper and cook for 5 minutes, then lower the heat and cook for about another 10–12 minutes or until just tender. Remove from the heat and set aside.

Third hurdle: Fire up the barbecue. Season the horse steaks and place on the grill. Cook for 3 minutes each side for rare, or longer if you prefer them medium or well done. Place the carrots, turnips, onions, courgette slices and potatoes on the grill until they are nicely seared.

Final furlong: Add the pink garlic to the frying pan with the remaining olive oil. Cook until it begins to turn golden, then add the cream. Bring to a simmer to thicken slightly. Season well and serve with the horse steaks and barbecued vegetables.

HORSEMEAT FACT

Around 70,000 horses were eaten during the
Siege of Paris in 1870-71.

IF THIS DISH WAS A HORSE IT WOULD BE

A spring foal. The freshest animal in the paddock.

Marinated Horse Kebabs
with Tomato Sauce

This mare-inated kebab gives your chunks of topside horse steak a dash of West Indian spice, so ideally you'll cook them over an open fire on a beach as dusk sets in after a scorching day. More realistically you'll need your full waterproofs and an umbrella to protect the fire.

SERVES 4

Ingredients:

   500g topside of horse, cut into cubes
   1 red pepper, cut into large chunks
   1–2 courgettes, cut into large chunks
   1 large aubergine, cut into large chunks

For the marinade:

   5 tbsp sunflower oil
   3 shallots, finely chopped
   3 large garlic cloves, crushed
   ½ tbsp West Indian curry powder
   sea salt, to taste

For the sauce:

   ½ tbsp olive oil
   1 garlic clove, cut into thin slivers
   1 x 400g tin chopped tomatoes
   1 tbsp clear honey
   ½ tbsp white wine vinegar
   1 tsp sugar

Method:

First hurdle: Combine the marinade ingredients in a large bowl and add the cubes of meat. Place in the fridge and marinate for at least 2 hours.

Second hurdle: Fire up the barbecue or preheat a grill to high. Use a slotted spoon to remove the chunks of meat from the marinade, and reserve the marinade.

Third hurdle: To make the sauce, heat the oil in a frying pan over a low to medium heat and fry the garlic until it starts to colour. Add the chopped tomatoes, honey, vinegar and sugar. Bring to the boil, then reduce the heat to medium and simmer for 30 minutes, stirring occasionally. Pour in the reserved marinade and simmer until reduced, to form a thick sauce. Pour the sauce into a blender and blitz until smooth, then return to the pan and keep warm.

Fourth hurdle: Thread the meat on to the skewers, alternating it with the vegetable chunks.

Final furlong: Place the kebabs on the barbecue or under the grill and cook for 5–10 minutes, turning a couple of times, until the meat is cooked through evenly and the vegetables are lightly charred around the edges. Serve with the tomato sauce.

IF THIS DISH WAS A HORSE IT WOULD BE

A Puerto Rican Paso Fino. Native to the Caribbean,
this breed can take the heat.

Horse Fillets with
Garlic Butter Sauce

The fillet steak is a gift from the horsey gods (there are a number to choose from, the most prominent being Roman goddess Epona). It's a prime cut, moist and tender just like its cattle-based relation, but less fatty. Surely it's time to give those poor bovines a break from the butcher?

SERVES 4

Ingredients:

120g butter
4 horse fillet steaks
8 garlic cloves, crushed
small bunch of flat-leaf parsley, leaves finely chopped
sea salt and freshly ground black pepper

Method:

First hurdle: Place half the butter in a frying pan over a medium to high heat. Season the steaks all over and when the butter is foaming, add the steaks to the pan and cook to your liking. (See the cooking time chart on page 12).

Second hurdle: Remove the steaks from the pan, cover and set aside in a warm place to rest while you make the sauce.

Final furlong: Add the remaining butter to the pan along with the garlic and parsley. Cook gently for 2 minutes, then check the seasoning. Pour the garlic butter sauce over the horse steaks to serve.

HORSEMEAT FACT

It's not just horse they eat on the Italian island of Sardinia, they've also got a taste for donkey.

IF THIS DISH WAS A HORSE IT WOULD BE

Sea the Stars. A racehorse cut from the finest stock.

HORSES FOR COURSES

Menu Suggestion: for a taste of the sea

Horse d'ouevres
Seared sgallops

Mane course
Haydock and chaps

Final furlong
Seabiscuit

DINING TIP

Eating a seahorse isn't really the done thing

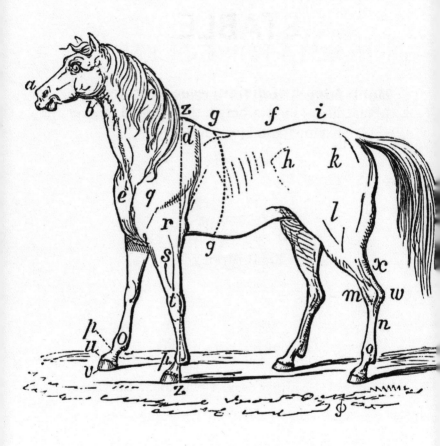

A
SOPHISTICATED
STABLE

'There is a touch of divinity even in brutes, and a special halo about a horse, that should forever exempt him from indignities.'

Herman Melville

The horse is a regal and elegant beast. Royal Ascot just wouldn't be the same if it were pigs doing the racing. Nobody would bother wearing a ridiculous fascinator to see that. So it stands to reason if you're going to eat such a refined animal, you should treat the meat with a bit of respect by indulging in some horsey haute-cuisine.

Horse Steak Tartare

To make sure this dish is the fine filly-dining experience you expect from a steak tartare, the horsemeat must be so fresh it has barely stopped neighing and is leaner than a size zero supermodel. You can vary the flavour of your tartare by adding very finely chopped parsley, chives or coriander; using lemon juice instead of Worcestershire sauce for a spot of extra acidity, or throwing a diced anchovy fillet into the mix to give it a salty tang. Accompany your raw horse with lightly toasted sourdough or fine-cut chips.

SERVES 4

Ingredients:

750g lean horse fillet

80g capers, rinsed

80g cornichons

80g shallots

2 tsp Worcestershire sauce, or to taste

Tabasco sauce, to taste

sea salt and freshly ground black pepper

4 egg yolks (shells reserved)

Method:

First hurdle: Trim the horse fillet to remove any fat and use a large, sharp knife to chop the meat as finely as possibly into tiny dice. This will take some time and is labour intensive, so if you have a stable hand, ask him to do it.

Second hurdle: Chop the capers, cornichons and shallots extremely finely and transfer to a mixing bowl. Add the diced horse fillet, Worcestershire and Tabasco sauces and season well. Mix all the ingredients until thoroughly combined.

Final furlong: To serve, arrange the tartare to form a circle on each plate and top each with an egg yolk in its shell.

HORSEMEAT FACT

French horsemeat butchers must display a golden horse head above their shop so that nobody is in any doubt what kind of flesh they are dealing in.

IF THIS DISH WAS A HORSE IT WOULD BE

A dressage horse. It looks good, but isn't to everyone's taste.

Horsemeat Carpaccio

Beef, veal, venison, tuna, salmon, they all regularly feature in carpaccio dishes so it seems a little churlish not to let horsemeat in on the action. As in a tartare the meat should be fresh from the field. Here it is thinly sliced and covered in a zingy lemon dressing.

SERVES 4

Ingredients:

400g piece best-quality topside horse fillet
juice of 2 lemons
3½ tbsp extra virgin olive oil
1 tbsp chopped chervil, plus extra leaves to garnish
100g Parmesan
sea salt and freshly ground black pepper

Method:

First hurdle: Wrap the meat in cling film and place in the freezer 1 hour before cooking. (This will partially freeze the meat and make it easier to slice thinly.)

Second hurdle: Mix the lemon juice in a bowl with the olive oil, chopped chervil and season with salt and pepper.

Third hurdle: Slice the meat extremely thinly using an electric knife. Alternatively, use a large sharp knife to cut the meat as finely as possibly, then place the slices between two pieces of greaseproof paper and use a rolling pin to roll it out as thinly as possible.

Fourth hurdle: Arrange the meat on a serving dish and use a pastry brush to coat with the marinade. Chill for 15 minutes.

Final furlong: Take the dish from the fridge. Use a vegetable peeler to cover the meat with shavings of Parmesan, then garnish with some fresh chervil leaves.

IF THIS DISH WAS A HORSE IT WOULD BE

Ribot. A great Italian stallion that won 16 races out of 16 in the 1950s.

Tournedos Rossini de Cheval

This recipe proves that horsemeat really can mix it in the highest social circles, combining with foodie royalty, foie gras and truffles, to create a deep and richly flavoured dish infused with luxury. Ideally, you will need to prepare the meat and the truffles the night before you plan to cook, to allow their flavours to mingle and deepen. And you should really eat this while wearing a crown and watching a horse you own run in a race named after you.

SERVES 4

Ingredients:

4 x 180g tournedos horse steaks
30g black truffle
1 tbsp rapeseed oil, plus a little extra for frying
100ml good-quality port
4 x 50g slices foie gras
10g butter, cubed, plus a little extra to finish
300ml veal or beef stock
few drops of lemon juice
sea salt and freshly ground black pepper
4 slices white bread, crusts removed, trimmed to size of the steaks
and lightly toasted, to serve

Method:

First hurdle: To prepare the meat, season the tournedos steaks well with salt and pepper and place in a large, lidded plastic container. Cut four very thin slices of the truffle and place on top of each steak, then drizzle with the oil. Cover with the lid and store overnight in the fridge. Cut the remaining truffle into thin slices. Place in a bowl with the port, cover with cling film and place overnight in the fridge as well.

Second hurdle: The following day, take out the steaks. Lift off the truffles and pat the steaks dry. Allow to return to room temperature before cooking. Strain the port, reserving it for later, and reserve the truffle strips.

Third hurdle: Place the foie gras slices in the freezer for 10 minutes while you cook the tournedos. Put the butter and a drop of oil in a heavy-based frying pan and heat until the butter begins to foam. Add the steaks and sear on a high heat for 2–3 minutes on each side, until browned well on the outside (they will remain rare and pink inside). Remove from the pan to a warmed plate and cover with foil to keep warm.

Fourth hurdle: To make the sauce, deglaze the frying pan with the reserved port, using a whisk to scrape any sticky residue off the bottom of the pan, then add the stock. Cook for about 2 minutes, until reduced. Strain the sauce through a sieve into a heatproof bowl, and add a small knob of butter.

Fifth hurdle: Heat a non-stick frying pan over a high heat and add the foie gras. Cook for 1 minute on each side, until nicely caramelised. Season, then remove from the pan to kitchen paper.

Sixth hurdle: Quickly reheat the sauce in the frying pan with the reserved slices of truffle and a couple of drops of lemon juice to taste. Add the tournedos steaks with their juices and spoon the sauce over them. Meanwhile, place the foie gras slices under the grill briefly to reheat.

Final furlong: To serve, arrange the lightly toasted bread on each plate. Place a steak on top of each slice and top that with a slice of foie gras. Spoon the sauce over the steaks, making sure each plate has a truffle slice.

HORSEMEAT FACT

Italians eat around 40,000 tonnes of horsemeat a year.

IF THIS DISH WAS A HORSE IT WOULD BE

Burmese. A black mare said to be a favourite of Queen Elizabeth's, who has probably eaten plenty of foie gras in her time.

Pepper-and-Herb-Crusted Foal Rib Steak

Add a peppery bite to the delicate flavour of your foal steak. It really gives it some hoof.

SERVES 4

Ingredients:

2 tbsp black peppercorns
2 tbsp white peppercorns

2 tbsp sea salt
5 sprigs of thyme, leaves only, finely chopped
5 sprigs of rosemary, leaves only, finely chopped
5 sprigs of tarragon, leaves only, finely chopped
5 sprigs of flat-leaf parsley, leaves only, finely chopped
2 x 450g foal rib steaks
2 tbsp olive oil
boiled new potatoes or baked potatoes, to serve
crème fraîche, to serve

Preheat the grill to high.

Method:

First hurdle: Pound the black and white peppercorns with the salt in a mortar. Add the chopped herbs and mix well to combine.

Second hurdle: Rub the steaks with the oil, then press them firmly into the pepper and herb mixture to give a generous and even herb coating on all sides.

Final furlong: Grill the steaks for 8 minutes each side. (Use tongs or a spatula to turn them gently so as not to damage the herb crust.) Serve with the potatoes and crème fraîche.

IF THIS DISH WAS A HORSE IT WOULD BE

An Appaloosa. Its speckled white and black coat gives the impression it has been rolled in a giant bowl of pepper.

Horse Wellington

*About the only thing the British and French can agree on is that
Provence is a lovely place to retire. Everything else is an argument
waiting to happen, including the Wellington. To the French the
unoriginal Brits have simply rebranded boeuf en croute. To the British
it's a patriotic pastry invented by the 1st Duke Of Wellington who
made a habit of showing Napoleonic France what's what. Either way
it's a great way to serve a piece of horse.*

SERVES 4

Ingredients:

knob of butter
1 banana shallot, finely chopped
1 garlic clove, crushed
50g mushrooms, cleaned and finely chopped
250g tinned foie gras
1 x 225g ready-rolled puff pastry sheet
1 x 800g piece horse fillet
1 egg, beaten
1 egg yolk, beaten

Preheat the oven to 180°C/Gas 4.

Method:

First hurdle: Melt the butter in a frying pan and fry the
shallot and garlic until translucent. Add the mushrooms and
cook for about five minutes, until soft. Season and set aside to
cool.

Second hurdle: Once cool, mix the foie gras with the mushroom mixture and beat until combined.

Third hurdle: Place the pastry sheet on a floured surface. Spread the mushroom paste down the middle of the pastry then place the horse fillet on top. Brush the edges of the pastry with the beaten egg, then fold the pastry over the meat to form a seam down the middle. Enclose the ends so that you have a neat parcel, making sure the pastry edges are sealed together well.

Fourth hurdle: Place the parcel on a baking sheet, sealed-side down. Brush the pastry with the beaten egg yolk and chill in the fridge for 10 minutes.

Final furlong: Cook the Wellington on the middle shelf of the oven for 25 minutes – this should give you medium-rare meat. Allow to rest for 10 minutes before serving thick slices with some green beans or steamed baby courgettes.

HORSEMEAT FACT

Nobody produces horsemeat like the Chinese, who churned out 168,000 tonnes of the stuff in 2009.

IF THIS DISH WAS A HORSE IT WOULD BE
Copenhagen. The Duke Of Wellington's horse, which he rode at the battle of Waterloo.

Roast Horse with Roquefort and Horseradish Sauce

Prepare for a stampede of big flavours. This dish doesn't prance gently about your taste buds it stomps all over them in an exhilarating manner. Horseradish, blue cheese, Dijon mustard: they're not ingredients that like to be tamed or held back. But this is one stampede you'll enjoy getting in the way of.

SERVES 4

Ingredients:

2 tbsp olive oil
1kg horse roast joint
Dijon mustard
sea salt and freshly ground black pepper

For the sauce:

45g blue cheese
3 tbsp soured cream
small bunch of chives, finely chopped
1½ tbsp horseradish sauce
1½ tbsp low-fat mayonnaise

Preheat the oven to 210°C/Gas 6.

Method:

First hurdle: Heat the oil in a frying pan over a medium to high heat. Sear the horse joint to brown all over, then remove from the pan.

Second hurdle: Place the joint in a roasting dish, season well with salt and pepper, then smear generously all over with the Dijon mustard.

Third hurdle: Place on the top shelf of the oven and cook for 10 minutes. Turn the oven down to 180°C/Gas 4 and cook according to how well you like your meat cooked (see page 12).

Remove from the oven and cover the meat loosely with kitchen foil while it rests for 10 minutes.

Final furlong: Mix the sauce ingredients together in a bowl, then transfer to a saucepan and bring to the boil. Carve the horse joint and serve with the sauce.

HORSEMEAT FACT

An old Mongolian wives' tale has it that eating horsemeat warms you up, which is probably why it's a favourite part of their winter diet.

IF THIS DISH WAS A HORSE IT WOULD BE

A mustang. There's something wild about these flavours.

Picula ad Caval
ITALIAN HORSE STEW

If you're a horse looking for a cultured city break here's a tip: give northern Italy a wide berth. You might just get eaten, because the people in these parts love nothing more than putting Ned in their nosebags. This stew recipe, originating in Piacenza near Parma, is just one of the many tasty ways they enjoy gobbling it.

SERVES 2

Ingredients:

2 tbsp olive oil
60g pancetta, diced
2 onions, finely chopped
60g minced horsemeat
125ml dry white wine
6 ripe tomatoes, skinned, deseeded and sliced
2 red chillies, deseeded and finely chopped
2 tbsp finely chopped fresh herbs (basil, oregano, and rosemary)
1 garlic clove, crushed or finely chopped
sea salt and freshly ground black pepper

Method:

First hurdle: Heat the oil in a small frying pan and fry the pancetta and onions over a medium heat for about 5–8 minutes, until the onion is golden, then add the horse mince and cook until it is brown, stirring to make sure it doesn't burn.

Final furlong: Add the white wine and bring to a simmer. Cover and cook for 1 hour. Add the tomatoes and chillies and continue to cook for 20 minutes. Sprinkle with the chopped mixed herbs and cook for a further 10 minutes. Season well and serve immediately.

HORSEMEAT FACT

Generating more than 80,000 tonnes per year, Mexico is the second largest producer of horsemeat in the world.

IF THIS DISH WAS A HORSE IT WOULD BE

From the hardy, northern Italian bred, Haflinger family.

Horse Entrecôtes in Whisky

Whisky improves almost any situation and since the entrecôte is also known as a Scotch fillet it seems appropriate to bring the pair together in one beautiful union, helped along by a luxurious cream sauce.

SERVES 4

Ingredients:

4 tbsp sunflower oil
4 rib or sirloin horse steaks (about 2cm thick)

4 tbsp whisky

280ml single cream

150ml beef stock

1–2 tsp green peppercorns

sea salt and freshly ground black pepper

green salad, to serve

sautéed potatoes, to serve

Method:

First hurdle: Heat the oil in a frying pan over a high heat and add the horse steaks. Cook for 2–3 minutes on each side for medium-rare, a minute more if you like your meat well done. Keep an eye on them to make sure they don't stick or burn.

Second hurdle: Pour the whisky over the steaks and cook for a couple of minutes. Add the cream and the stock along with the green peppercorns. Season well.

Final furlong: Remove from the heat and serve immediately with a green salad and sautéed potatoes.

IF THIS DISH WAS A HORSE IT WOULD BE

A Highland pony. As Scottish as Whisky.

Polish Horsemeat Pâté

*The Poles are fond of all things equine – the feats of their cavalry
have passed into legend – and this delicacy will remind all your Polish
friends of home. You'll need a kitchen equipped with a meat grinder to
get it just right.*

SERVES 8–10

Ingredients:

1.5kg horse joint, deboned

100g parsley

2 bay leaves

about 3 litres vegetable stock (a cube or bouillon powder is fine)

800g potatoes, peeled and boiled

100g butter

½ onion, finely chopped

1 tsp freshly grated nutmeg

1 tsp allspice

1 tsp ground black or white pepper

sea salt

Pre-heat the oven to 200°C/Gas 6.

Method:

First hurdle: Rinse the horsemeat then place in a large pot
with the parsley and bay leaves and enough stock to cover.
Bring to the boil and simmer for 2–3 hours or until tender.

Second hurdle: Remove the meat and parsley from the stock, then strain it. Pass the meat, boiled potatoes and parsley through a mincer several times to mince it finely. Alternatively, place in a food processor and process to fine mince. Transfer to a large mixing bowl.

Third hurdle: Heat the butter in a frying pan over a medium heat and fry the onion until golden, then add both the butter and onion to the meat mixture. Add the spices and seasoning and knead well using your hands. If the pâté is too dry, add a little of the strained cooking stock.

Fifth hurdle: Grease a large baking tin, add the pâté mixture and smooth down with a spoon.

Final furlong: Bake in the hot oven for approximately 30 minutes or until the top has browned and the pâté is heated through.

IF THIS DISH WAS A HORSE IT WOULD BE
A Wielkopolski. Little known outside Poland but much loved by the locals.

Hay-Smoked Horse Tenderloin
with Dauphinoise Potatoes

Hay-smoking has enjoyed a bit of a gastronomic revival in recent years and there's no reason you shouldn't join in at home. It's a pretty simple technique but will have foodie friends braying with delight especially if horsemeat, which already has a hint of grassiness to it, is the main ingredient. If you really want to impress, cook it all over apple-wood embers on an open fire.

SERVES 4

Ingredients:
For the hay-smoked horse:
1kg horse tenderloin
½ bag of eating hay
olive oil

For the dauphinoise potatoes:
500g Maris Piper potatoes
1 garlic clove
knob of butter
300ml milk
300ml double cream
salt and freshly ground black pepper

Preheat the oven to 180°C/Gas 4.

Method:
First hurdle: For the dauphinoise, peel and thinly slice the potatoes.

Second hurdle: Peel and halve the garlic clove and rub each half around the inside of a shallow baking dish, then rub the dish with some butter before layering the potatoes. Season with salt and pepper as you go.

Third hurdle: Combine the milk and cream and pour over the potato layers. Then pop them in the oven for 1 hour and 45 minutes.

Fourth hurdle: Turn the oven up to 200°C/Gas 6, then heat some oil in a cast iron casserole dish on a stove and brown the horsemeat all over.

Fifth hurdle: Remove the horsemeat, then add a little more oil and the hay. When it begins to smoke, add the horsemeat, cover the dish and put it in the oven for 20 minutes.

Final furlong: Remove the meat from the hay and leave it to rest for 10 minutes before serving with the dauphinoise potatoes.

HORSEMEAT FACT

Belgium imported almost 12 million euros worth of horsemeat from Mexico in 2011.

IF THIS DISH WAS A HORSE IT WOULD BE

A draft horse. They're big and they've got a big appetite for hay.

HORSES FOR COURSES

Menu Suggestion: For something quick and easy

HORSE D'OUEVRES

Frankelfurters

MANE COURSE

Pepperpony pizza

FINAL FURLONG

Appaloosa pie and ice cream

DINING TIP:

To avoid indigestion avoid eating fast food at a gallop

HORSEMEAT SUPPLIERS

Ask your local butchers if they are able to source good-quality horsemeat. Alternatively, two online retailers in the UK will deliver horsemeat straight to your door.

Kezie Foods
Burnhouse Farm
Berwickshire
Duns
TD11 3TT
Tel: 01361 884 006
www.keziefoods.co.uk
info@kezie.com

Exotic Meats UK
Tel: 08450 948414
www.exoticmeats.co.uk

And if you'd like to try 100% horsemeat jerky, order online from: http://cowleysfinefood.com